READ TOGETHER

All About
Polar Bears

EDventure
LEARNING

How to Use This Book

This book is part of our Read Together series, a collection of books designed to be enjoyed by a young reader paired with a more experienced reader, such as a parent, grandparent, or older sibling. Take turns reading out loud together.

 The pages on the left side are meant for the younger reader. These pages use short, simple sentences and larger print. They are marked at the bottom of the page with the symbol shown at left.

The right-side pages are for the older reader. They contain paragraphs with longer sentences and more complex vocabulary. These pages are marked at the bottom of the page with the symbol shown at right.

Shared reading helps new readers gain confidence. It's also a great way for all ages to bond over books. We hope you enjoy this book as you Read Together.

Printed in the United States of America
Paperback ISBN: 978-1-64824-018-8

EDventure Learning LLC
5601 State Route 31 #1296
Clay, NY 13039

www.edventurelearning.com
Email us at hello@edventurelearning.com

Table of Contents

What Polar Bears Look Like . . . .   p. 4

Where Polar Bears Live . . . .   p. 12

What Polar Bears Do . . . .   p. 18

Glossary   . . . .   p. 28

Index and Credits   . . . .   p. 29

What Polar Bears Look Like

They are white.

Their thick coats of fur keep them warm. The white color acts like **camouflage**, helping them blend in with the snow.

Underneath all that fur, polar bears have black skin. This helps them take in more heat from the sun. They also have a thick layer of fat to keep them warm.

They are very big.

Polar bears are the largest bears in the world. When they are standing on all four legs, they are around 4-5 feet (1.2-1.5 m) tall. However, when they stand up on their hind legs, they can be up to 10 feet (3 m) tall!

They have big paws.

Polar bears walk on four legs, and each has a large, padded paw. Their paws even have fur on the bottom to help them keep warm and to stop them from slipping on the ice.

Their eyes have
three lids.

Polar bears have a third, clear eyelid. This lets him see underwater (like having built-in goggles). The extra eyelid also helps protect their eyes from blowing snow.

Where Polar Bears Live

They live in the Arctic.

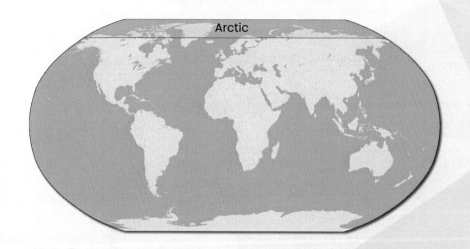

Arctic

Polar bears live north of the Arctic Circle. The largest number of polar bears live in Canada. Polar bears can also be found in parts of Russia, Greenland, Norway, and the United States.

They live where it is cold.

The Arctic has long, very cold winters and short, cool summers. In the winter, the Arctic region has average temperatures around –30°F (–34°C). In the summer, temperatures usually hover around the freezing point 32°F (0°C).

They live near water.

Polar bears live mainly on ice sheets that sit on top of the cold Arctic waters. In the summer, some of these ice sheets melt, forcing polar bears to live on the mainland until the water freezes again in the fall.

What Polar Bears Do

Polar bears swim.

These bears are very strong swimmers. Their big front paws are slightly webbed, so they act like paddles to help the bears swim. Polar bears can swim very long distances.

They hunt for food.

Polar bears are **carnivores**, which means they only eat meat. Seals are a polar bear's main source of food. Polar bears hunt by waiting near the water's edge or near a hole in the ice for seals to come up for air. When a seal comes up, the polar bear tries to grab it.

They like to stay clean.

Keeping their fur clean helps it stay white so they can blend into the snow. Their fur also works best to keep them warm when it is clean and not matted down with dirt. Polar bears bathe by diving into the water or rolling around in the snow.

They have babies
called **cubs**.

Polar bear mothers usually give birth to two cubs at a time in a den they dig in the snow. Cubs are usually born in the winter and stay in the den with their mother until spring. When they are born, the cubs are tiny. They weigh as little as 1 pound (0.5 kg).

They live alone.

Polar bears do not live in groups like some animals do. Males spend almost all of their time alone. Females live alone or with their cubs. Cubs stay with their mother until they are around 2 years old. In the wild, polar bears live to be 20-25 years old.

Glossary

Camouflage
A way for an animal to blend in with its surroundings

Carnivore
Animal that eats only meat

Cub
Baby polar bear

Index

A

Arctic, 12-15, 17

Appearance, 4-11, 19, 25

C

Camouflage, 5, 23, 28

Cub, 24-25, 27-28

F

Food, 20-21

H

Habitat, 12-17

Hunting, 20-21

S

Size, 6-7, 27

Swimming, 11, 18-19

Credits

Check out these other titles in the Read Together series!

All About Camels

All About Cheetahs

All About Giraffes

All About Elephants

All About Kangaroos

Keep in touch!

FOLLOW US ON SOCIAL MEDIA

   @edventurelearning

 www.edventurelearning.com

 Want freebies? Email us at **hello@edventurelearning.com** with the subject "Read Together" to join our newsletter and we'll send you free printables to keep the learning going!

All About Lions

All About Penguins

All About Polar Bears

All About Tigers

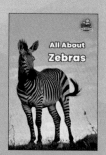

All About Zebras

Made in United States
North Haven, CT
27 May 2022

19606839R00018